LEADING ACADEMIC DISCUSSIONS

What Every University Student Needs to Know

Robyn Brinks Lockwood

University of Michigan Press
Ann Arbor

ISBN-13: 978-0-472-03795-7 (print)
ISBN-13: 978-0-472-12898-3 (ebook)

2024   2023   2022   2021   4   3   2   1

▰ Acknowledgments

The word *leader* can be interpreted many ways depending on the context, ranging from guide to companion, coach to pilot, and engineer to mentor. In a discussion, a leader serves many roles—guiding, coaching, engineering, and mentoring among them. In the 12-plus years I have been teaching Academic Discussion at Stanford University, I have seen the great leadership potential my students have. I commend them for honing their discussion skills so they will be able to lead not only academic discussions but also professional communications and activities, such as meetings, conference sessions, panel discussions, or company/team projects. I am grateful for their attendance, participation, and initiative in my class. I would like to thank Connie Rylance and the Fall 2020 Academic Discussions students for piloting these materials and for providing valuable feedback. They have made this a better book. I also want to acknowledge those who have served as my guides, companions, coaches, pilots, engineers, and mentors. Thanks to Kelly Sippell, my editor at University of Michigan Press, for playing whatever role I needed as I developed this manuscript. Thanks to my parents, Virgil and June; my husband, John; and my brother Tim, for never ceasing to be both leaders and cheerleaders for me. And, I dedicate this to Darrin and Nathan, my nephews, who I know will be great team players and leaders.

■ Contents

Introduction

For more than 12 years, I have taught an academic discussion course at Stanford University. I could never find a book that adequately taught students how to participate in and lead discussions. My students had already taken a variety of speaking courses and could traverse a basic conversation. Many had already studied pronunciation and knew the sounds and blends of the sound system. They had studied listening skills and were already entrenched in classes at the university or had numerous opportunities for listening practice with their textbooks, so comprehending the general content they heard was fine. Some had even already taken a presentation course, so they could give a speech in front of the class if given the time to prepare. But my academic discussion course requires a little bit of each of these, so no one book would work. And, I didn't need a big book. I needed a brief book that focused on just the skills and language students would need to use and recognize to be good leaders, allowing enough class time for actual discussion practice. Additionally, to be a good discussion leader, you need to be a good participant. Therefore, I needed to create materials that allowed students to first become good participants and then good leaders.

In addition to students participating and eventually even leading discussions, students need to realize that speaking in person is not the only type of communicating they will have to do. Many of my students were being challenged by phone interviews for their internships and even more were faced with online interviews using a variety of platforms.

Teaching Speaking Online

In the spring of 2020, students around the world were also taking all their classes online, which changed the way we teach but did not necessarily change our course objectives. When I received the alert on a Friday night near the end of the quarter that the course would finish online, I had one weekend to figure out how my groups were going to lead discussions online. Rather than using the name placards I gave each student to set in front of them in class, students would now have to rely on the Zoom name that appeared on screen. Instead of projecting their PowerPoint to the screen in the classroom and being situated at the front of the room, they would have to share their screens and their Zoom "square" would be wherever it appeared on screen. (At that time, Zoom did not allow users to move "squares." More recent Zoom updates allow this so students can "sit" by each other or the teacher can arrange students.)

My students were troopers. We did the best we could. But I realized that students still need to participate in class and in discussions whether they were online or not. The ability to participate and lead on screen is vital to students' success. Even when we teach in a classroom in person again, the ability to communicate online needs to be content we practice because online conferences, interviews, meetings, classes, and other types of discussions or interactions are likely to continue.

With so many different types of projects and discussions possible, I found one thing that students really worried about most—leading a discussion. It seemed that that was the book to write. If students are taught how to **lead** discussions, they would, by default, also learn and practice the skills and language they needed to **manage** discussions as participants. Thus, *Leading Academic Discussions: What Every University Student Needs to Know* was born.

My next step in the development of this book stemmed from deciding what someone needs to know in order to lead a discussion. When I worked on the first book in this series, *Office Hours: What Every University Student Needs to Know*, I discovered that an office hour meeting has five **moves** and that each of those moves contains certain language the participants use to accomplish the goal or objective of that particular move. For example, Move 4 in an office hour, Negotiating

Academic Business, includes asking for help, asking for advice, clarifying, and making excuses (among others). Knowing the moves and the appropriate language can lead to a successful office hour interaction. There are certain words and phrases one needs to ask for help (and successfully get it). There are ways to make an excuse that are better received than others. Could the same be true of a discussion? Are there moves? Is there certain language associated with each move? Can knowing this language lead all students to being better leaders and better participants? The short answer is yes, although it was less obvious what those moves are and certainly more overlap or blending of the moves.

In summary, this book evolved from years' worth of handouts, interviews, and focus groups with students, conversations with colleagues, scripts of discussions from corpora, recordings of group discussions from my classes, information from former students about their discussions and meetings in their academic and professional settings, and observation of discussions in a variety of departments across campus. Most recently, it included information from my students about what they were experiencing with interactions in their classes once they were all online. After reviewing my notes, I outlined six moves that leaders need to navigate through in a discussion and some language they need to both deliver (as a leader) and understand (from the participants) to lead a successful academic discussion or professional speech event whether that be in person or online. As the six moves took shape, this book evolved. I hope students and instructors will find it useful on campus. However, meetings and discussions in professional settings are likely to mirror these same six moves, so I believe this book can propel students into leadership beyond academia and into the workforce, no matter what field they choose. If you like this book, you can thank the many students who took my Academic Discussion class at Stanford University because they kept telling me to write this book.

Let the discussion begin!

A Note about Using This Book

This book will teach you about discussions. You will learn the characteristics of a discussion, different types of academic discussions, and the roles people play in those discussions. You will also study some of the factors that might change the dynamic of a discussion, such as gender or content. Then the book will introduce you to the six "moves" that discussions include and the language you will need as you go through each of those six parts—both as a participant in the discussion and as a leader of a group.

While discussions are heavily reliant on words, they are also influenced and affected by other verbal cues, such as pronunciation, stress, pitch, or tone. Speakers need to both notice and use these cues to make their messages clear to other participants. Discussions are more than words and verbal cues. There are other factors that do not involve words at all, yet these other types of communication also influence the communication. Therefore, a section on non-verbal communication, such as gestures, facial expressions, and eye contact, among others, has been included.

To be a good discussion leader, you must also be a good participant. Even if you never need or want to lead a discussion, you will need the language and knowledge in this book to be a good participant. You will learn that even if you are not the appointed leader, most participants often serve as a leader at different points during a discussion, and they may not even realize it. You also want to develop leadership skills for use beyond the classroom. To help you develop these skills, this book includes So You Want to Lead a Discussion boxes, which are designed for students to notice features of participants'—and their own—speaking styles and goals. By observing and analyzing them, you can improve your skills as a participant in academic discussions and become good leaders in academic and professional settings. If students do not aspire to being TAs, discussion leaders, or project leads, this content can be skipped.

The book includes several group activities and rubrics that instructors may use to provide grades or feedback. Robert's Rules of Order, which are formal rules often adopted by organizations, businesses, and governments, are included for your reference. Consider implementing these during one of the discussions in class to try the language and style.

Six video clips of mock discussions (available for free online) accompany this book (www.press.umich. edu/elt/compsite/leading). The word *mock*, by definition, lets you know that these clips are not authentic classroom discussions, but they are included for analysis and critical thinking. The scripts are included with activities that focus students on using the language taught in the book, noticing the moves of a discussion, thinking about better ways to say things, recognizing pronunciation features, observing the different roles participants play, evaluating wording or structure, and/ or simply learning new vocabulary and idioms.

1

What Is a Discussion?

Why Are Discussions So Important in College?

Discussion is an important part of the class-room regardless of discipline. Participating in discussions can help you process the content from class because you are actively rather than just passively listening to information. Discussion allows you to connect with and critically think about the content, helping you to apply the content to problems or situations, understand other perspectives, and express your own opinions and support those opinions. Discussion also helps you be more engaged, keeps you awake, and helps you better remember and retain content, which can then lead to better understanding and maybe even better test scores and grades. Asking questions during discussion provides clarification, so you know if you really understood the content or someone else's opinion and/or offers you the chance to ask for clarification.

Asking for clarification is not a bad thing. It shows that you are listening and that you are engaged with the class.

Participating in online discussions is just as important, especially since online communication is becoming more prevalent for job interviews, conference presentations, and workplace meetings. There are some good reasons to practice online discussions even if you also have in-person classes or meetings with your fellow students, professors, or supervisors. Sometimes being online might actually be less intimidating if you are worried about speaking up in person. Many online platforms have a chat box and course management systems have a discussion strand, so some discussions are written rather than spoken. The advantages to these are that they might be less intimidating, and they might be more thoughtful. Participants can more carefully think about their wording since these might be recorded permanently. The written discussions also offer more opinions and ideas since everyone is better able to participate. Many online courses still meet synchronously, so discussions will be live just as they were in class. The instructor may call on you to speak or break you into small groups (that will take place in a breakout room) just as would happen in a traditional classroom. Learning the language you will need and the general practice of discussion will help you in either setting.

Characteristics of a Discussion

Before someone can lead or even participate in a discussion, it is important to know what a discussion is. Most people would agree that a discussion is the action of talking about something, which seems simple enough. However, we listen to people talking all the time, but we would not always say that everything we hear is a discussion. Conversations, for example, are generally not considered discussions, at least not all of them. Though there are some traits that can apply to both, we should try to make some type of distinction.

Think about conversations you have recently had with a friend or family member. It is likely that those conversations were generally less formal. For example, a conversation with your brother or sister or with friends will be less formal than one you have with your teacher, advisor, boss, or research group members. That's not to say you cannot speak informally with teacher or advisor. Some of the formality might stem from how well you know the person. Graduate students who have worked with their advisors for many years are more comfortable speaking less formally than an incoming college freshman or first-year graduate student who is meeting their advisor for the first time.

Discussions are more precise or have a more specific purpose, perhaps to reach a decision, to debate a topic, or to exchange ideas. **Conversations** might be about less formal topics, like movies, restaurants, or gossip. It should be noted, however, that people often have long discussions about a movie, during a critique about its merits perhaps; in fact, a discussion is also defined as a detailed "treatment" of a particular piece of writing or a specific speech. Therefore, discussions may dwell on one topic for a longer period of time and might require more effort. Topics in conversations are sometimes less formal, so they might not dwell on any one subject for long and they could change quickly from one topic to another without any notice or smooth transition. Of course, an easy distinction might be that conversations are more relaxing and fun whereas discussions are not. Of course, so much depends on the topic. There is no reason why you cannot enjoy an academic discussion or dislike a conversation, depending on the factors that might affect an interaction.

One way to distinguish between the two might be to examine the synonyms for *discussion* versus those for *conversation.*

- Synonyms or related words for **discussion**: *conference, debate, consultation, deliberation, powwow, seminar, symposium, negotiation, argument, dispute, parlay, skull session, colloquy*
- Synonyms or related words for **conversation**: *talk, dialogue, tête-à-tête, chat, heart-to-heart, confab, chitchat, rap, bull session, convo, jaw, gab, yarn*

These lists show that discussions sound more serious and formal and conversations are more fun and informal. But so much depends on other factors, such as who the participants are, the setting, the topic, or even the age, gender, and status of the participants. First let's focus on some examples of how discussions and conversations are the same. Conversations and discussions share some similarities. In both, there is a mutual exchange of words between two or more people. Conversations tend to be smaller (between fewer people), but you might go to dinner party, especially a formal party like a wedding, where there are eight or 10 people at one table and where you all have participate in the conversation. Discussions are usually done as part of a larger group, but two people can engage in a very in-depth, serious discussion about a topic such as politics. For example, a student and an advisor can discuss the merits of a course when planning a student's schedule.

Both discussions and conversations often use the same **discourse markers** (words or phrases that function as signposts to signal listeners what the speaker means and help organize the discourse or spoken language). Discourse markers will be covered in depth in 2: The Structure, or Moves, of a Discussion, but one example is *I think,* which is a common discourse marker for expressing opinions. Speakers use this discourse marker to signal that the information that follows is not a fact but the speaker's own opinion. This marker is common in both conversations and discussions.

With these similarities overlapping, it is useful to note that there are some words that can be used to describe both discussions and conversations.

■ Synonyms or related words for **discussion** and **conversation**: *talk, exchange, dialogue, discourse*

Types of Academic Discussions

There are still some very large lecture-style classes with hundreds of students. In those lecture halls, discussion is less likely to happen, though the professor may still open the floor to questions. While it is true that the smaller a class is, the more likely it is there will be more discussion, do not be lulled into thinking that big classes do not expect participation. The students may be divided into groups for discussion with TAs or the professor moving from group to group. Discussion might take place as you work with a group to develop a project or conduct research, it might take place as a graduate student shares his or her progress, it might be in the form of Q&A after another student gives an oral presentation, or it may occur in some other iteration. Discussion happens all the time!

One way to notice how much discussion is taking place is by beginning to recognize types of interactions that may occur in a classroom. This list is dependent on the class, major, or field of study since teachers, courses, or fields may have different conventions. For example, reading discussions are very common in history or literature. A reading discussion means that everyone reads the same article or book and then everyone discusses it in class or perhaps in small groups if the class is large. These may even happen outside of the classroom; students may set up times to meet after class, over dinner, or in the evenings.

Some types of academic discussions are:

- class discussion
  - can be led by instructor or students
  - can be open (anyone talks anytime) or closed (each person is given an opportunity to speak)
  - can be broken into smaller groups or include the whole class
  - can be spontaneous or planned
- panel
- debate
- case study (everyone discusses a specific case)
- book/reading (everyone discusses the assigned book, article, or other reading)
- staff, research group, committee, or team meeting

Factors Changing the Dynamic of a Discussion

Despite the similarities, there are some differences between discussions and conversations. As mentioned earlier, a variety of factors distinguish the two. The same factors that affect any social interaction also change the dynamic of a more formal discussion: relationship, age, gender, status, time, location, content, and context

Look at a few examples:

Relationship (friends, family, roommates, classmates, colleagues, etc.): Do you talk to your friends the same way you talk to classmates you don't know as well?

Age: Do you talk to talk to your grandmother the same way you talk to your sister or brother? Do you talk to an elder professor the same way you talk to a classmate?

Gender: Do you talk to your female friends the same way you talk to your male friends?

Status: Do you talk to your boss the same way you talk to your classmate?

Time: Do you talk the same way in the morning as you do at night after dinner?

Location: Do you talk the same way in class as you do at a party?

Content: Do you talk the same way about dinner plans the same way you talk about politics?

Context: Do you talk the same way during a debate about politics in class as you do during a conversation about politics with a good friend?

For a more in-depth study of factors affecting social interaction, see *Speaking in Social Contexts* (Lockwood, 2018).

Focus on one factor for a moment, in particular: status or position. Consider a meeting with a professor and two students. The professor might lead that discussion with the students in the participant role. Status can influence the leadership, but purpose and other factors might also affect the dynamic in such a way that status is not a factor. Consider a research group meeting with eight students and one professor. You might think that the professor leads and the students participate. However, if this is a graduate program, students might take turns leading and it will not matter that one person at the table is a professor. This example shows how drastically only one factor can change the dynamic. Just imagine how several factors at play at the same time can change things.

Roles in a Discussion

The two primary roles in a discussion are leader and participants. A **leader** is generally responsible for several tasks.

Leaders or Moderators

- start the discussion
- make sure everyone participates
- keep the discussion moving (avoids delays or silences)

- manage the time (or assigns a timekeeper)
- keep the peace
- distribute work
- assign roles
- distribute, collect, and submit any materials
- end the discussion

Participants have their own set of responsibilities.

General Participants

- respond as needed through the discussion
  - Note: You may think this sounds easy, but it is actually harder than you think. You must respond often and appropriately. Being a participant does NOT mean being an observer!

A leader may also be responsible for other tasks, such as "goal tending" or "summarizing," or he or she may assign responsibility for some of those other tasks. Participants might even volunteer or conduct some of these other tasks on their own. Participants can take on one or more roles during a discussion.

Goaltenders

- read (and maybe announces) the directions
- remain aware of the situation or questions to be addressed

- help ensure instructions, situations, or questions are being addressed
- are vigilant about the purpose and goal
- prioritize and/or help the team not get bogged down in details

Summarizers

- explain instructions, situations, or questions in different words
- make sure everyone understands the purpose and goal
- paraphrase what others say when necessary
- play a key role in overall comprehension for participants
- clarify when someone does not understand

Statisticians or Record Keepers

- take notes
- write numbers, facts, and results
- record the final outcome
- report the group's results to the rest of the class
- keep records for future discussions

Shared Tasks (Everyone)

- listens actively
- presents ideas and opinions
- supports ideas and opinions with facts, examples, details, reasons, and the like

- solicits ideas and opinions from others
  - *According to an article I read in an IEEE journal....*
  - *I read NASA's website and it said....*
  - *Our professor said....*
- explores new topics, situations, or potential
- elaborates on other's points
- plays devil's advocate (supports an opposing or unpopular view for the sake of argument to make sure that the topic is thoroughly discussed from every angle)
- asks questions
- listens
  - <u>Note</u>: Listening is sometimes even more important than talking, especially for the leader.

Discussions can have a clear leader, such as a classroom discussion that is led by the instructor, or can be **closed,** where all participants are guaranteed a turn that is often granted or ensured by the leader. The participants then assume or share other roles through the discussion. The roles can change at different meetings or even during the same meeting or discussion. In other words, everyone may be the leader at some point. Sometimes it is better to assign roles, but they may also fall into place naturally. Also bear in mind that not all the roles are required to be filled. Sometimes only some of the roles will be filled. Other times, roles may be blended or subdivided; for example, the statistician may record all the results but there may be a "reporter" that reports those to the rest of the class. So much is dependent upon the factors, most especially the content.

TASK 1

Think about an interaction you have had in the past. Answer the questions.

o Setting: Describe what the discussion or conversation was for (class, club, organization, meeting, job, enjoyment, etc.).
o Leader: Was there one distinct leader? Who was it?
o Participants: Who else was there? Who were they (classmates, friends, coworkers, etc.)? How many people participated?
o Topics: What did you talk about?
o Type: Can you identify if it was open or closed? Was it planned in advance or did it happen spontaneously?

Talk about the experience you described with a partner or small group. Answer these questions.

o Did you speak a lot? Why or why not?
o When did you choose to keep quiet?
o When did you interrupt? Why or why didn't you interrupt?
o Have you thought about the fact that people take on different roles in a discussion? Did this happen in the experience you described here? What about at another time? What did you notice?

TASK 2

Read each situation. Imagine you are participating in a discussion. Talk about how these situations might change the dynamic for you.

You are participating in a discussion:

1. with all members of the opposite gender as you

2. with most members of the same gender as you

3. with all members about the same age

4. with members who are all older than you

5. with your classmates

6. with your classmates and your instructor

7. with a 10 a.m. meeting time

8. with a discussion over happy hour

9. in your classroom

10. in your professor's office

11. at a dinner party

12. about a sensitive topic like politics

13. about a disagreement about the direction in which to move a project forward

14. about a reading required for class

Consider different combinations of the situations or make up one of your own. Work with a partner. Combine two or three to create a new situation. How does that change your participation? The participants' reactions? Take notes and be prepared to share those with the rest of the class.

TASK 3

Work with a group. Read this true story.

> Janice Burke is a math teacher in Mesa, Arizona.
> When she was giving a test to her 5th grade class
> one day, something unexpected happened. This
> occurrence was so strange that it interrupted
> the math test. The teacher is OK now, and so are
> the students. However, when asked about this
> occurrence, one of the pupils, 10-year-old Jamie
> Morgan said, "We got real scared." (Situation from:
> Folse, K.S., 1996, *Discussion Starters*. University of Michigan Press.)

You have 10 minutes to discuss this situation with your group. What
are at least five possible occurrences that interrupted the math test?

After 10 minutes, ask one group member to share the group's list.
Each group is granted five minutes to briefly discuss the items on
its list. There will be a five-minute Q&A session for groups to ask
questions of the other groups.

After the Q&A, return to your original group. You have another
10 minutes to discuss your original list and the other lists. Make a
final choice. Your final answer may be one of your original ideas,
an idea from another group, a combination of ideas, or a new
idea. What occurrence interrupted the math test? Present your
answer to the other groups.

So You Want to Lead a Discussion

- Did each group member play a specific role? Who did what? Were roles shared? Were tasks shared?

- Who played more of one role than another? Was there a clear leader?

- What was your main role? Did you also play any other roles?

- Did all members participate? If not, why not? Did everyone play an active role in making the final decision? Why or why not?

- How can you improve your role? How can you become a leader (or better leader)? How can you become more involved?

- What discussion skills do you most want to learn or improve?

2

The Structure, or Moves, of a Discussion

Discussions, especially open discussions, may seem to have little or no structure, as if anyone or everyone is talking at the same time or in no order. Although it may appear there is no organization, there is some overarching structure to the discussion. This structure is often unfamiliar to or overlooked by participants, which becomes rapidly apparent when students do not use the proper phrasing or do not say anything at all. When the moves are missing, a discussion may not proceed as well as it could have, and participants may feel disappointed after the discussion. It is important to (1) be familiar with the parts and (2) to know the language—verbal and non-verbal—you should use as you progress from part to part. A leader moves a discussion through six moves. The six moves are:

1. Starting the Discussion
   ↓
2. Getting All Participants Involved
   ↕
3. Managing Participants and Controlling Content
   ↕
4. Keeping the Discussion Going
   ↕
5. Clarifying and Confirming Consensus
   ↕
6. Summarizing and Closing

Note where the arrows between each move point both ways. Why? As much as we would like for discussions to neatly move from one step to another, the process is more fluid and often depends on the factors. After the leader starts the discussion, maybe Move 2 is not needed because there are only four people and it is a closed discussion in which each person will have a turn. Maybe the leader will have to repeat Move 3 if there is one participant who has not talked much and needs to be called on and later there is another participant who is talking too much. Move 5 may occur more than once, especially if the discussion has more than one purpose or goal. You will see how this can happen as we learn about each of the six moves.

Move 1: Starting the Discussion

Calling to Order

You would think that Move 1 is the first thing to happen. That is true to a degree. The actual discussion does not always formally begin. Be aware that there is sometimes talking before the actual discussion. As people enter the room, there are greetings and perhaps even some small talk. If there is coffee or refreshments, people may ask about other classes, how your weekend was, or even offer a compliment as they are getting a drink or some food. You can review some social interaction language to help you participate in conversations before the official discussion, such as greetings, introductions, complimenting, and small talk.

You will notice that Move 1 is at the top of the moves and has only an arrow pointing downward. Move 1 must happen first to "officially" start the discussion. A leader will say something like:

Is everyone ready to get started?
Are we ready to begin?
Let's get started.
Everyone, we'd better get busy.

In more formal situations, a leader might execute Move 1 with:

I'd like to call this meeting to order.
We need to begin.
It's 3:00. Time for us to begin.
My watch says it's time to get started.
We don't have much time today, so we'd better start.

Providing Scope or Focus

Once the leader has the attention of the participants and everyone is situated (around the table, in their chairs, etc.) and settled (has their coffee and notebooks/computers), there is usually a short pause or silence. The leader can then proceed to the second part of Move 1—giving the scope or focus. This part of the move focuses the participants. When possible, the leader:

- specifies (or reviews) the topic and purpose of the discussion:
  - Topic: *Today we need to discuss* The Great Gatsby *that everyone was assigned to read for our English class.*
  - Purpose: *The instructor asked that we discuss what made this novel an American classic.*
- narrows the topic if necessary:
  - *Since there are many reasons why this novel has made its mark in U.S. literature, I thought maybe we can focus on themes.*
- offers a starting question or springboard (avoid yes/no questions or questions with one-word answers <u>and</u> avoid unanswerable or overwhelming open-ended questions):
  - *In what ways does Fitzgerald convey the theme of [love, wealth, isolation, the American Dream, mortality] as seen in* The Great Gatsby?

- ▪ maintains a list of questions, arguments, or topics that arise and/or can be used if the discussion lags:
  - *We've talked a lot about the theme of [mortality], what about the theme of [wealth]? Which characters exemplify wealth?*
  - *We've talked a lot about the theme of wealth, what other themes do you think Fitzgerald includes?*
  - *Can someone who is not from a wealthy background really be accepted or blend in with the old money crowd in the novel? Why or why not?*
- ▪ brings participants "into the know" so that everyone has the background they need (if they don't have it or if you'd like to prepare more):
  - *I have copies of the first chapter if we need them.*
  - *I prepared a slide with the main themes critics agree Fitzgerald covers. Maybe we can pick one of these to kick off our discussion.*
  - *I wrote a list of the key criticisms levied at the novel.*

■ outlines any constraints or concerns (time limits, sensitive topics, respect for others' opinions, keeping the discussion fair and polite):

- *We only have an hour today.*
- *Critics sometimes disagree on [a point], so let's make sure we respect everyone's opinions today.*

TASK 4

Answer these questions.

What would you do if:

1. you were starting a meeting at a business?

2. you were starting a study group?

3. you were starting a discussion about a book, article, or case study?

4. you were starting a discussion about a team project?

5. everyone was talking and it was loud?

6. everyone was already seated and ready?

So You Want to Lead a Discussion

Walk through the steps a good leader follows to prepare for a discussion. Use the example for the discussion about a novel to guide you. Can you develop a topic of your choice as necessary to be a strong leader?

Topic:

Purpose (goal or objective of discussion):

Narrowed Topic:

Starting Question:

Extra Questions (2–5):

Background Knowledge for Participants:

Constraints or Concerns:

Move 2: Getting All Participants Involved

After starting the discussion, the next move is to actually get the participants to speak. Notice the bi-directional arrow between this move and Moves 1 and 3. A leader may have to do this several times, such as opening the floor at the beginning or re-focusing when the topic has strayed off course or a new topic or subtopic is starting.

Sometimes the leader will want to open the floor to for anyone to start. There are certain words or phrases that open discussions. Use something like this to open the floor.

So, who would like to start?

Does anyone want to comment on [the article we were assigned]?

What did everyone think of [the book]?

Who has an idea [for our project]?

What do you all think caused [the results we got in the lab]?

Let's list some ideas [for conference abstracts].

Once the original discussion is started, a leader might begin mentioning people specifically by name or bring up a specific point.

Who wants to add on to what Abdoul said?

What do you think about Miguel's point?

Does anyone have any other answers to the question?

Can anyone answer Jeena's question?

TASK 5

Discuss these questions with a partner or small group.

1. How do you feel when a leader opens the discussion to anyone? Do you speak first? Do you defer to someone else?

2. How do you feel when a leader mentions someone by name? How do you feel if you are the person named?

So You Want to Lead a Discussion

- What can you do if no one begins after you open the floor?

- How can you learn everyone's names? What strategies can you use?

- What factors should you consider when calling people by name?

Brainstorming

One way to get everyone involved is to hold a brainstorming session. Brainstorming is a strategy groups can use to produce ideas. In general, brainstorming is helpful to a leader because it opens the floor to all participants, and it produces a lot of ideas. Brainstorming is also helpful to participants because it is open to everyone. It can be very helpful if there the leader gives a **trigger**—a topic or question to start the session.

GUIDELINES FOR A BRAINSTORMING SESSION

- Set a time limit to accumulate ideas. The focus at the beginning is **quantity** not **quality**.
- Say anything that comes to mind. The leader or record keeper makes a list of ALL ideas, no matter how crazy, irrelevant, or surprising.
- Make no judgments. All ideas are added to the list without comment.
- Say ideas quickly as they come to mind. Don't worry about grammar or pronunciation.
- Everyone should be involved if at all possible.
- Build on previous ideas.
- When time is up, begin discussing the ideas on the list. The focus now is **quality** not **quantity**.
- Cross out any ideas that don't fit, won't work, or are redundant.
- Circle any ideas that seem most useful or interesting. Depending on the purpose of your discussion, try to narrow this down to the Top 3 or Top 5.

TASK 6

Hold a five-minute brainstorming session with a small group. The trigger is: What are some ways for new students to make friends at your place of study or work? After five minutes, shift the focus from quantity to quality. Take ten minutes to discuss the ideas and choose the top three.

ROUND ROBIN BRAINSTORMING

Another popular way to brainstorm is round robin or chain brainstorming. In this method, all participants are required to participate. Envision a group of six students sitting around a table. In round robin brainstorming, one person says their idea first, then the person sitting next to that person says an idea, and so on. You can't skip a turn and the next person can't say anything out out of turn. One advantage of this is that everyone has the opportunity to participate; quieter members get to talk and more dominant personalities don't take over. One drawback is that you may sacrifice some of the quantity if someone gets stuck.

TASK 7

Hold a five-minute round robin brainstorming session with a small group. The trigger is: There are many topics or issues citizens want their government to address. What are the most important? After five minutes, shift the focus from quantity to quality. Take ten minutes to discuss the ideas and choose the top three.

So You Want to Lead a Discussion

- How many ideas did you have in the general brain-storming session? In the round robin brainstorming session? To what can you attribute these numbers?

- The text suggests that brainstorming has advantages and disadvantages. What are some advantages of each type of brainstorming? What are some disadvantages of each type?

Brainstorming	Advantages	Disadvantages
General		
Round Robin		

- In which circumstances might starting a discussion with brainstorming be helpful? Can you think of any circumstances in which brainstorming might not work?

Active Listening

In any discussion, leaders and participants need to actively listen. They need to be able to express opinions (and recognize others' opinions), agree, and disagree, and they need to be able to do those things politely and respectfully. Active listening also means they need to clarify, paraphrase, and summarize. This language will be covered in other moves. It is a good idea to use and recognize the most common discourse markers for expressing opinions, agreeing, and disagreeing since those can occur throughout the discussions and in more than one move.

For any set of discourse markers, remember that any words or phrases within that set share the same general meaning and the same function. They let you know the speaker's purpose. They also help speakers connect their comment to those that came before theirs. And, they help the discussion move smoothly.

Review these lists.

STATING OPINIONS

As far as I'm concerned....	*I think....*
As for me....	*In my opinion....*
As I see it....	*It seems to me....*
I believe....	*Personally speaking....*
I consider....	*To my mind....*
I suppose....	

AGREEING

Exactly.	*That's a good point.*
Good idea.	*That's just what I wanted to say.*
I agree.	*That's right.*
I'm down with that.	*That's so true.*
I'm with you.	*Yeah. / Yes.*
Makes sense.	
Of course	

AGREEING IN PART

*Although I agree with most of what you said, I can't
 agree with what you said about....*
*By and large, I agree/see your point/accept your
 view....*
I agree in principle, but....
I agree on the whole, but....
That may be true, but....
I see what you mean, but....
I have some sympathy with your position, but....

DISAGREEING

But....	*I'm not convinced by your argument.*
Don't you think that...?	*I'm not sure about that.*
I beg to differ.	*I'm not sure I agree that....*
I disagree.	*I'm sorry/I'm afraid I disagree....*
I don't think so.	*No way.*
I must take issue with what you said.	*That's ridiculous/crazy.*

Note that discourse markers do not really hold any content; the content is in the statement that follows. Together they create a contribution that can be discussed. The discourse marker alone only tells you the speaker's *function* or *purpose* of the content it precedes.

Discourse Marker + Content = Contribution to Discussion

(opinion) +   (content)
I think + gun control is a topic our politicians need to debate.

(agreement) +   (content)
I agree + gun control is a topic our politicians need to discuss.

(disagree) +   (content)
I disagree. + I think the most important topic is immigration.

(partial agreement) +   (opinion) +   (content)
Although gun control is important, I think the more important issue is immigration.

TASK 8

Practice using the phrases to discuss these topics with a partner.

- autonomous vehicles
- the best [author, president, class, food, movie...]
- getting a graduate degree
- cell phone usage
- political issue [capital punishment, immigration, abortion, healthcare, etc.]

A practice dialogue might look like this:

Person A gives an opinion.

Person B asks why Person A has that opinion.

Person A supports the opinion.

Person B agrees or disagrees and states his or her own opinion.

Person A asks why Person B has that opinion.

Person B supports the opinion.

Person A agrees or disagrees.

TASK 9

Hold a group discussion. Read the situation and come up with a solution. Use opinion, agreeing, and disagreeing language. Be prepared to share your results with other groups.

Situation: Your academic department just received $100,000 dollars from a wealthy alumni donor. How should the money be spent?

So You Want to Lead a Discussion

While words and phrases within a set of discourse markers share the same general meaning and function, they can vary in formality or directness. Which phrases in each category are more or less formal? More or less direct? Which factors might help a leader determine when to use different discourse markers?

Opinions:

Agreeing:

Disagreeing:

Can you think of any other words or phrases or have you heard/observed any other words or phrases for each category?

Opinions:

Agreeing:

Disagreeing:

Talking about Data

In some discussions, you may have to cite or support statements with data. In formal talks, you may actually be able to show figures, tables, and charts. For a good discussion on data commentary in writing, read *Academic Writing for Graduate Students* (Swales & Feak, 2012). Some of this language can be useful in discussion. Actually showing data is not always possible in a discussion, but you can still talk about results.

Review the phrasing presented. Notice how you need to let listeners know opinions or ideas are/held by the majority or minority or if they are divided.

The majority of....	*There was not a clear majority.*	*Only a small number....*
Most respondents....	*Results were divided among options.*	*A minority of interviewees....*

Make sure you:

- make generalizations: *From these results, we can generalize that....*
- let us know you are surprised: *I was surprised to find out that....*
- reveal contradictions: *Although I expected the survey to reveal [THIS], I actually learned....*
- draw conclusions: *The fact that [THIS] proves that....*
- indicate movement: *There was a rise/increase/ improvement/jump OR There was a fall/decrease/ decline/drop.*

- indicate stability: *Research shows this trend is remaining constant/is stable/leveled off/ plateaued.*
- indicate things are still changing: *I don't think we can focus on this result because things are still fluctuating/changing/moving.*
- indicate the lowest levels: *We can't make that our business idea. The sales bottomed out/struck a low.*
- indicate the highest level: *We can't make that our business idea. The sales already peaked/reached their highest point.*

TASK 10

Go to the U.S. Census Bureau website at www.census.gov. Click on Access Local Data and pick a state, county, city, town, or zip code that you want details about. Choose a place you are interested in learning more about. Present a few statements about your data to your classmates. If you have time, compile the data in a chart or graph to show as a visual aid during your discussion practice.

Move 3: Managing Participants and Controlling Content

Move 3 can be challenging. Not only does a leader need to juggle the participants, who may be of different personalities and communication styles, to make sure everyone has a chance to speak, but they also need to control the content, keeping the discussion on topic so the objective or purpose is met.

Managing Participants

One thing to consider is the different language styles and tones people have. Let's divide them into three broad groups: formal, neutral, informal. Consider these examples of what someone with each language style or tone might say if they disagreed with something that was said.

> Formal: *I'm very sorry, but I must disagree. I'm afraid your idea is not the most important one.*
> Neutral: *I'm afraid I disagree. I think we need to consider other ideas.*
> Informal: *What? No. That's not right. We need another idea.*

TASK 11

Decide for each situation whether the language style or tone you would use is formal, neutral, or informal.

When you finish, compare your answers with a classmate or with a small group. Discuss any differences. Share what factors might affect a change in your answer.

1. asking a professor to edit your research paper

2. asking your group members to change the time of your discussion

3. asking your group members to change the topic you already settled on for your project

4. being interviewed for an internship or job

5. having a meeting with a professor and the two students in your project group

6. presenting at a conference

7. holding a meeting with your research group

8. holding a meeting with a club

9. working on an assignment for class with your roommate

10. during office hours with a professor whose class you are taking for the first time

TASK 12

For each situation discuss what you would do with a group or partner.

1. You need to take a phone call in the middle of class.

2. You need to miss the next class meeting.

3. You attend a group happy hour and you are the first student to arrive after three professors.

4. You are shopping at the grocery store and you see your advisor.

5. You need to ask a professor if you can join his/her lab.

6. You want to get a few students together to form a study group.

So You Want to Lead a Discussion

- What do you think your primary language style or tone is?

- Which language styles or tones are easiest to work with? Which are the hardest to work with?

- Think about a time that you have had to work with someone who had a different language style than you. How did you adapt?

Let's next think about varying personalities. Sometimes there are people who don't talk at all; other times there are people who talk too much. As a leader, it might be helpful to have someone who talks a lot because the discussion keeps moving, but it might be frustrating to others who would like to jump in but are unable to. Certainly their language style or tone—formal, neutral, or informal—also affects the dynamic. Someone who is talking a lot might not bother someone as much if they are formal. In any case, it is important that everyone participate. Some key words and phrases you can use to involve everyone are listed.

INVOLVING QUIET PARTICIPANTS

Xiao, what do you think?
John, how do you feel about the ideas posed so far?
What do you suggest, Eva?
Max, do you have anything to add?
How about you, Margarita?

CONTROLLING (OVER)TALKATIVE PARTICIPANTS

Let's see what some others have to say.

Josef, you have a good point. Why don't we see what some other people think?

Angelina has given us some food for thought. How about someone else chime in now?

Let me ask you to pause there. We should get input from everyone else.

Note: While it adds a personal touch to use personal names, the names are not required. You can use non-verbal communication (gestures or eye contact) to call on specific participants.

TASK 13

Discuss these questions.

1. Have you ever been part of a discussion that has one person who is very outspoken and talks more than everyone else? Have you ever been that person?

2. How do you feel if you want to say something but are unable to jump in?

Controlling Content

In addition to managing the different language styles and participant personalities, you also need to control the content. While it doesn't sound hard to do, it can be challenging because you have to let others in the group know that something they have said is irrelevant, their priorities are not in line with the group, or their suggestions may not be accepted. You also need to make sure that everyone is taking turns. To do all of these, you have to interrupt or help others interrupt so everyone has a chance to be heard. Review the lists of discourse markers that can serve these purposes.

STATING IRRELEVANCE (THE CONTENT IS OFF-TOPIC)

How is that related to...?

How is that relevant to our discussion?

I don't see how that fits into our discussion.

I don't see the relevancy/ relationship to....

I don't think that has anything to do with....

I don't think that is really related to....

I fail to see the relevancy of _____ (that).

Is that really germane to our discussion?

That doesn't have anything to do with this.

That is taking us off track.

That really has nothing to do with what we are talking about.

That's a (completely) different topic.

That's an interesting idea, but it raises a different point.

That's not going to help here.

What does that have to do with it/anything?

What does that have to do with the topic?

Why mention that? It isn't related.

Reviewing, Restating, or Determining Priorities (focusing people on what is or should be most important)

A vital consideration is....
Our purpose is....
The highest priority for our discussion is....
The main thing is....
The most important/key task to complete is....
We can't lose sight of our main goal.

Managing Suggestions

Make suggestions using phrases such as:

Consider this....   *We might say....*
Here's an idea....   *What about...?*
How about...?   *What do you think about...?*
I suggest....   *Why don't we...?*
Perhaps we could....

Ways to doubt, accept, or reject a suggestion are listed:

Doubting a Suggestion	Accepting a Suggestion	Rejecting a Suggestion
I'm not really sure.	*Yes/Yeah, okay.*	*No. I don't think so.*
I don't know. Maybe.	*That's a great idea.*	*That won't work.*
Well...I guess maybe.	*Sounds good.*	*I can't go along with....*
In theory....	*Works for me.*	*No way.*

Taking Turns and Getting Attention

Can I ask a question?
Can I make a suggestion?
Could I say something here?
I have a point (I'd like) to make.
*I have a question (I'd like to ask)/a suggestion (I'd like
    to make)/something (I'd like to say).*
I haven't had a chance to talk. Let me have a turn.
Not everyone has had a turn. Let's go around the table.

TASK 14

What can you say in each of these situations?

1. Carl changes the topic unexpectedly.

2. Everyone needs to leave for another class in about 10 minutes.

3. Mikhail is talking so fast that no one can really understand his point or his pronunciation.

4. It has taken Viktor two full minutes to explain something and he doesn't seem close to finishing.

5. No one seems to have any idea what Grace is talking about.

6. You can't get everyone's attention to start the discussion.

7. Silence falls about 30 minutes into the discussion.

8. Magda, who is very shy, hasn't said anything yet.

9. Katerina is talking so quietly that no one can hear her.

10. Martin is having trouble interrupting and he clearly has something to add.

TASK 15

Read the situation and consider your ranking. Using the chart on the next page, use Column 1 for your own ranking. Then work with your group to create a ranking in Column 3. Use all the language studied in this unit.

> Imagine that you are part of a space exploration mission flying from a space station orbiting the Moon to a base on the Moon itself. An instrument malfunction causes you to crash on the Moon on the daylight side about 120 kilometers from the base. Your spacecraft is in need of repair and your survival depends upon reaching the Moon base as soon as possible. Of the fifteen items that were not damaged in the crash of your spacecraft, which would be most important for the 120 kilometer trip? Rank the items from most important (#1) to least important (#15).
>
> Items: signal flares; self-inflating raft that uses carbon dioxide canisters for inflation; two .45-caliber pistols; parachute silk; food concentrate; box of matches; solar-powered heating unit; stellar map of the Moon's constellations; 18 meters (50 feet) of nylon rope; magnetic compass; 15 liters (5 gallons) of water; first-aid kit containing needles for vitamins, medicine, etc., that will fit a special aperture in spacesuits; solar-powered FM walkie-talkie; two tanks of oxygen; one case of powdered milk.

From: https://starchild.gsfc.nasa.gov/docs/StarChild/space_level2/activity/problems_space.html

Examples of language you might hear:

A: *I think we should take X first because we may need it.*

B: *Wait. That's not going to help here. We need a lot of things. I suggest taking....*

A: *You're right. But I still want to take X. We may need it to survive until we reach the base.*

B: *True. But our priority shouldn't be something that we may need....*

Your Independent Ranking	Available Items to Take from the Spaceship	Your Consensus Group Ranking
	box of matches	
	food concentrate	
	50 feet of nylon rope	
	parachute silk	
	solar-powered heating unit	
	two .45-caliber pistols	
	one case of dehydrated milk	
	two 100-pound tanks of oxygen	
	stellar map (of the moon's constellations)	
	self-inflating life raft	
	magnetic compass	
	five gallons of water	
	signal flares	
	first-aid kit containing injection needles	
	solar-powered FM receiver-transmitter	

Now look at the answers in Appendix 1. Transfer your ranking and your group ranking. Compute your error points by figuring out how many points difference there was between your ranking and NASA's. For example, if you ranked something as 3, but NASA ranks it as 5, your error point total for that row is 2. Only the difference matters, not whether it is above or below NASA's ranking. Then total the error points.

So You Want to Lead a Discussion

- Was your independent ranking better or worse than your group ranking?

- Why might a group ranking be better than an individual ranking?

- Why might an individual ranking be better than a group ranking?

There are many functions you may have to perform as a leader or even as a participant. Some of these are harder than others. For example, it can be challenging to interrupt another speaker. But if you don't interrupt, another person might hold the floor for too long and you might not be able to speak. Similarly, if you're leading, others in your group might get frustrated if they don't get to participate. You may also want to hold the floor yourself or need to get the floor back if someone has interrupted you.

Interrupting

Interrupters often apologize first by saying *Excuse me* or *(I'm) Sorry* at the beginning of the interruption. Some examples are included in the list. Apologizing before adding new content (the reason for the interruption) is common and can soothe hurt feelings.

APOLOGIZING/INTERRUPTING

Can I say something here?
Excuse me for interrupting, but....
Excuse me, but I'm going to stop you there.
Excuse me, but....
Hold on a second....
I can add to that.
I can comment on that.
I need to stop you (for a minute/there)....
If I could interrupt (for a second/here)....
Let me jump in here.
Oh, my idea piggybacks....
Sorry to cut in.
Sorry to interrupt, but....
Sorry, but....
Wait.

KEEPING YOUR TURN (AFTER AN INTERRUPTION)
OR PREVENTING INTERRUPTIONS

I have only one (more) thought....
I just want to say one thing about this....
I'd just like to/I just wanna finish this one thing.
If you could wait for a just a sec, I'm just about to finish.
If you let me say just one more thing, then I'll be finished.
It won't take me long to explain this.
Lemme just finish my point, okay?
Oh, I'm almost done. One more second?

GETTING YOUR TURN BACK (AFTER AN INTERRUPTION)

Anyway....
Before you jumped in, I was saying....
Getting back to what I wanted to say....
Going back to what I was saying....
In any case....
So, as I was saying....
Soooo....
Where was I?

TASK 16

Work with a group. Each person will have a chance to choose a topic and start a discussion. The others in the group will continue to interrupt using one of the phrases listed on pages 52–54 and/or asking a question. The speaker will get their turn back and bring it back to the original topic. Take turns.

Example:

> A: *Last night I watched the debates on television.*
>
> B: *Excuse me, but what debates are you talking about?*
>
> A: *The presidential debates. Anyway, it was interesting.*
>
> C: *Wait. I have a question. Who was debating?*
>
> A: *There were six debaters....*

TASK 17

Discuss these questions with a partner or small group.

1. What happens if you leave out the apology at the beginning?

2. When, where, who do you interrupt? When, where, who do you <u>not</u> interrupt?

So You Want to Lead a Discussion

- Which is harder to do—controlling people or content? Why do you feel that way?

- Besides the actual discourse markers, how can tone of voice or volume affect the dynamics of controlling people and content?

- Are there other discourse markers that can be added to the lists to help with Move 3?

Move 4: Keeping the Discussion Going

Like Move 3, Move 4 can be challenging. Think of a time that you were part of a discussion and there was an awkward period of silence or a class in which the professor asked a question and no one answered. How can you keep the discussion going, especially if you are the leader and you are responsible for the discussion moving forward?

In general, the leader can say something like:

*Are there any more comments before we tackle the
     next point?*
Maybe we should go on to the next point.
Perhaps we can come back to that a little later.
*We seem to be getting bogged down. Let's move
     forward with another point. We can revisit this
     later.*
We only have 20 minutes left, so we'd better move on.
*We only have 5 minutes left, so let's summarize where
     we are.*

Some strategies can help keep the discussion
moving:

- adding information to content already in
  play
- getting more information about a particular
  point to keep people talking
- asking probing questions to elicit more
  discussion
- countering to spur argument or more
  discussion

Scan each list of discourse markers. Then use them
to complete the tasks.

ADDING INFORMATION TO CONTENT ALREADY IN PLAY

Another thing/idea to add is....
I think it's important for us to know that....
I think it's important to add that....
I'd like to add something....
Let's not forget that....
One more thing we need to consider is....
We also need to take into account that....

GETTING MORE INFORMATION ABOUT A PARTICULAR POINT TO KEEP PEOPLE TALKING

Can you be more specific?
Could you explain more about...?
How can you say that?
How do you mean?
What do you mean by that?
What leads you to that idea/conclusion?
What makes you say that?
Why do you think so?

ASKING PROBING QUESTIONS TO ELICIT MORE DISCUSSION

Are you assuming that...?
Can you give some more details?
Have you given any thought to...?
I wonder if you've considered....
I'd like to ask you about....
I'm curious about....
What evidence do you have?

COUNTERING TO SPUR ARGUMENT OR MORE DISCUSSION

Can't you see that....   *Nonetheless....*
Even so....   *Still and all....*
Granted....   *The fact of the matter is....*
In any case....   *You must recognize that....*

TASK 18

Find a partner. Imagine you are going to follow through on one of the situations. State your intention to your partner. Your partner will try to get more information or ask a probing question. Explain your reasons. Your partner will try to counter so that you will not follow through.

Situations:

1. You're sick of all the homework and exams required to get your degree. You are going to quit school and travel around another country instead.

2. You could not get into any of the classes you wanted and all your classes start at 8 AM. You are going to skip classes next week to catch up on sleep.

3. You have too much email, too much homework, too much research, and you do not have enough hours in the day to get it all done. You are going to focus on email and pay someone to do your homework and research for you.

4. Your car broke down, but you do not want to cancel your road trip to see Las Vegas, so you're going to hitchhike there instead.

5. The university accidentally charged you for 10 hours' worth of tuition instead of 12. You decide to keep the money and spend it on clothes.

6. You got a speeding ticket and are due in court. You decide to skip the court date.

So You Want to Lead a Discussion	
Prepare for a discussion with your classmates. Anticipate some opinions people will have. What are some questions you can use to ask for more information, get more information about those specific points, and counter those specific points?	
Topic	
Anticipated opinions	
Questions to ask for more information about those anticipated opinions	
Questions to get more information about why people have their opinions	
Questions to counter the opinions (the opposite viewpoints)	

Move 5: Clarifying and Confirming Consensus

The first part of Move 5, clarifying, might happen during Moves 2, 3, and 4 as well. It may even happen during Move 1 when the leader mentions the focus or objective of the discussion and someone does not understand and they want the topic reworded. The second part of Move 5, confirming consensus, almost always has one instance that occurs near the very end of the discussion. However, it, too, might happen during Moves 2, 3, or 4, if there is more than one purpose, objective, or topic.

Clarifying

Clarifying is a good strategy to use when you did not understand or you want to make sure you did understand. You also need to clarify when you are the leader and are making sure that all participants are understanding the content. You can simply ask for clarification or say you do not understand. Or, you can try a more advanced, but often more effective strategy—paraphrasing.

STATING YOU DON'T UNDERSTAND/
ASKING FOR CLARIFICATION

> *Can you repeat that?*
> *Could you explain that again?*
> *I didn't follow what you said.*
> *I didn't get your last point. Could you go over it again?*
> *I don't get it.*
> *I have no idea what you mean.*
> *I'm afraid I am not quite clear what you mean by that.*
> *I'm afraid no one understood.*
> *I'm not sure I understand what you mean.*
> *I'm not sure what you're getting at.*
> *I'm sorry, but I just don't understand.*
> *What?*

Paraphrasing and Responding

The person asking for clarification uses a discourse marker and attempts a paraphrase from Column 1 of the chart. The speaker can respond in the affirmative or negative with discourse markers such as those in Columns 2 and 3 of the chart. You might notice how many more negative options there are, leading us to believe that people often paraphrase incorrectly!

Paraphrase	Affirmative Response from the Speaker	Negative Response from the Speaker
Correct me if I'm wrong, but are you saying...?	*Yes./Yep./Yeah.*	*That's not exactly what I mean.*
I didn't follow what you said about....	*Exactly.*	*No, let me put it another way.*
Am I correct in assuming that you mean...?	*That's right.*	*Not exactly. Basically, what I'm trying to say is....*
When you say [X], do you mean that [X]?	*You got it.*	*I guess I haven't made myself clear. Let me try again....*
Would I be correct in saying that you think...?	*Right.*	*Maybe I can make it clearer by....*
You mean....		*I'm afraid there is a misunderstanding.*
What you're saying is...?		*I mean....*
So, you are telling us that....		*In other words....*

ASKING IF EVERYONE UNDERSTANDS

Any questions?
Do you see what I [or participant name] mean(s)?
Does everyone understand?
Does that make sense to everyone?
Is that clear?

PARAPHRASING FOR SOMEONE ELSE

Sungmin said….
What Li means is….
I believe Celine's point is….
I think Geoff feels…. Is/Isn't that right, Geoff?
Let me see if I understand for the group. You mean….

TASK 19

Imagine you were participating in or leading a panel. Look at these quotes from a panel that discussed cyber awareness and resilience. Paraphrase the question the leader asked and the answers and statements panelists and audience members posed.

Question: Can system attributes be effectively randomized to take away the advantage of the malicious attacker?

Paraphrase:

Panelist: One of the things related to this is fixed points in a network. So if we make it easy to plug in application and hardware, we make it easy for attack. We need to minimize constraints. Hacks into systems give us a clue as to what the architecture should be. So the first step should be to get constraints down to a small number and then put randomization around them.

We are being hindered more and more by not being able to find the relevant stuff. We have compartmentalized our systems to prevent security breaches and then in turn tried to connect these. We need to think about interactions across different levels.

Paraphrase:

Audience Member 1: Randomization is just one aspect. Whenever you randomize, you must always have one thing that is fixed. This does not necessarily make the attacker's job more difficult but it may make programming more difficult.

Paraphrase:

Audience Member 2: From his experience, there aren't too many cases that can't be overcome. Our goal is to make their lives more difficult.

Paraphrase:

Samples from: https://secure.inl.gov/isrcs2009/docs/ISRCS_Panel_Discussion_Notes.pdf

---

So You Want to Lead a Discussion

- What is challenging about paraphrasing?

- What strategies have you learned from writing classes that might be helpful when you need to paraphrase during a discussion?

- In your opinion, is it okay for the leader to say they didn't understand what was said? Why or why not? What might happen if you don't understand and attempt to paraphrase?

Confirming Consensus

Throughout a discussion, but almost always at the end of a discussion, the leader might try to confirm the solution or proposed solution, especially if time is running short.

Some possible phrasing includes:

Can everyone live with...?
Can we all agree that...?
Do some of the ideas/solutions overlap? Maybe we can combine them.
I know not everyone will be happy, but can we move forward with...?
Is there anything we can agree on?
Is there anything we can settle on?
So, it sounds like we have decided....
There probably isn't one perfect solution, but does [XXX] sound like something we can all accept?
What do all the ideas share?
What's one idea we can agree on?

Sometimes you may have the chance to revisit a solution at a later time:

> *Let's table this for now. Give it some thought and let's*
> *meet again tomorrow.*
> *The solution isn't as good as it can be, but let's take it*
> *for now and revisit it at our next meeting.*
> *We may have to compromise. Give the ideas we have*
> *some thought and bring an open mind to our next*
> *meeting. We'll try again.*

Notice that one phrase suggest tabling something. *To table* something means "to postpone" something. It can mean to postpone indefinitely, but usually it is postponed until the next meeting. This phrasing is common in Robert's Rules of Order. Robert's Rules of Order are more formal. These rules are the most widely used rules for parliamentary procedure. They were started by a man named Henry Martyn Robert, who was in the Army during a time in the United States (mid to late 19th century) when people of many nationalities, ethnicities, and cultures were coming together. He felt meetings were chaotic and they were all handled differently. Robert felt it would be helpful to have some rules common for any type of meeting. He looked at the government rules and adapted those for use in other settings. Hence, Robert's Rules of Order came to be. He published the first book in 1876. Now, the book is in its 11th edition and has over 600 pages. While not often used in academic discussions, Robert's Rules are used in a variety of organizations, including academic or educational organizations. To study them well, you would need to read the book, but to participate in meetings that adopt these rules, you really only need a brief overview of the "motions" and language people use during a meeting adhering to Robert's Rules. You can find detailed information at Robert's Rules website (https://www.robertsrules.com) and a myriad of shorter versions and cheat sheets by conducting an online search. A brief overview posted by NOAA is included in Appendix 2 of this textbook.

TASK 20

Work with three other students. Take turns leading the discussion with each member leading the discussion about one of the locations. At the end of your discussion, propose one location. Clarify and paraphrase throughout the discussion. Use Robert's Rules of Order if you would like to practice the parliamentary procedure.

Many disciplines have an honor society. An honor society is a group that encourages good grades and leadership within the discipline. Some examples include Sigma Tau Delta (English), Tau Beta Pi (Engineering), and Beta Beta Beta or TriBeta (Biology). Your team has been tasked with choosing a location for the next conference for your major's honor society. Each person in your group will lead a discussion on one of these places. Take some notes on each place before the discussion begins if you are not familiar with them.

> Choice 1: Las Vegas, Nevada
> Choice 2: New York City, New York
> Choice 3: Orlando, Florida
> Choice 4: Denver, Colorado

So You Want to Lead a Discussion

- What are advantages to Robert's Rules of Order? What are disadvantages?

- What can you do to get consensus? What should the leader to if there is no consensus but your professor or boss is expecting an answer?

Move 6: Summarizing and Closing

The transition between Moves 5 and 6 may be difficult to distinguish. Some may argue that confirming consensus is part of summarizing. And that's fine. Even if it is included as part of Move 6, this move is often short and to the point.

First you may have to signal everyone that the discussion needs to end:

Everyone, we're almost out of time....
Time is almost over....
We're about out of time....
I know we could keep talking, but we do need a solution before we leave....
Our decision is due at 5:30 and it's already 5:00.
It's time to wrap up.
We need to close/stop for today.

Then you should summarize the discussion. Review the paraphrasing language and the confirming consensus language because it can be used again here. Some other phrases are:

Then we all agree that....
To sum up, we've decided....
So, I think we've got it then. We all want....
Our final [proposal] is....

It is always nice to thank everyone for their participation.

Thanks, Everyone.
Good discussion. We got a lot of great ideas to work with.
I really appreciate everyone's contributions.

So You Want to Lead a Discussion

- Have you ever had a leader who didn't end with a Move 6? What was that like? How did you feel?

- What can happen if there is no Move 6?

- If a leader doesn't offer an expression of appreciation at the end, how do you feel?

3

Other Discussion Considerations

Non-verbal communication is extremely important in any kind of interaction, whether it be social, academic, or professional. Non-verbal cues play a role in academic discussions and are used by leaders and participants alike. Leaders can use them to help gauge how participants are feeling and drive the discussion. Participants can use non-verbal language to reinforce their words, but they can also use it to replace words. For example, if someone is having trouble interrupting or getting attention, they could raise their hand.

Some non-verbal language is negative and can negatively impact the discussion. Think about someone who rolls their eyes when you suggest an idea they don't like or when someone just sits slouched in their seat without making eye contact, conveying the message that they are unengaged or uninterested. Use non-verbal cues to your advantage, not to your detriment.

Types of Non-Verbal Communication

Gestures

When you use gestures, you use parts of your body, such as hands, arms, or shoulders in place of or in conjunction with your verbal communication.

Type of Gesture	Function Conveyed
Shrugging your shoulders Hands out with palms up	Lack of knowledge
Thumbs up Nodding yes	Agreement Confirming Clarifying
Thumbs down Shaking head no	Disagreement Shock or surprise
Raising your hand	Getting attention Interrupting Adding information
Pointing	Bringing someone into the discussion Soliciting input
Holding up your hand (palm out)	Stopping the discussion (Time's up) Interrupting
Slouching or sitting back	Boredom Relaxation (less likely)
Sitting up straight	Paying attention
Fingers or hand moving in circle	Encouraging speaker

TASK 21

Think of other gestures you have used or noticed during an interaction. How would you complete the chart? Then compare your chart with a partner. Add any other new ideas to your chart.

Type of Gesture	Function Conveyed

Facial Expressions

Facial expressions are another way to enhance communication. The two most common are happiness (smiling) and sadness (frowning). But, like gestures, some may be detrimental. Facial expressions are very telling. Others that might be useful to recognize during an academic discussion include surprise or shock, frustration, support, disagreement, or even anger and are shown in the chart.

Facial Expression	Physical Signs
Happiness	Smiling (mouth corners raised)
Sadness	Frowning (mouth corners lowered)
Surprise or shock	Rounded mouth (mouth open, jaw dropped) Eyebrows raised Eyes widened Tipped head
Frustration	Upper lip raised Wrinkled forehead or nose Clenched teeth
Dislike	Rolling eyes Looking "down your nose" Wrinkled nose
Support	Smiling (accompanied by nodding)
Disagreement	Frowning (accompanied by shaking head) Lips pulled up on one side Eyes partly closed Smirking One eyebrow raised Sideways glance Grimacing Wincing
Anger	Closed mouth (lips in straight line) Eyebrows lowered Sneering Pouting Squinting
Concern	Pursed lips
Interest	Quizzical (slightly tipped head, hand on chin)

Note: People sometimes say someone has a poker face. A poker face shows no expression. You cannot tell how the person feels or what the person is thinking.

It's certainly a benefit if you are actually playing poker. No one can tell how you feel about the cards you are holding during the game. However, it could be detrimental when participating in an academic discussion or might even be interpreted as you not caring about the discussion.

Eye Contact

Eye contact in some cultures, such as U.S. culture, is very important. What constitutes as eye contact? Eye contact is when two people look into each other's eyes at the same time. Looking into the other person's eyes is a sign of respect, but it also shows that you are actively listening and care about what the person is saying. It shows you are paying attention, but it also helps you better convey your own meanings and understand the other person because you can see their facial expressions and lip movements. It can be challenging, especially if you are from a culture in which it is respectful to not look people with higher status in the eye or from Asian cultures in which children are sometimes taught to look below the person's eyes as a sign of respect for that person's role such as a teacher or boss.

TASK 22

Practice each of the type of gesture and facial expression. Then write a few notes about which ones are easiest to understand, which ones are more challenging to understand, which ones you think are most important, and which ones you most want to improve.

TASK 23

Divide the class into two teams. With your team, convey each of these messages non-verbally. Then take turns conveying them, in random order, to the other team. Can they guess your message correctly?

I want to say something.

Hello.

I have to leave soon.

I don't know what you mean.

I disagree.

What!? I don't believe that.

I'm thinking.

Give me a second.

Stop what you're saying.

You're crazy!

So You Want to Lead a Discussion

- Do you or will you use non-verbal communication when you are the leader? What about when you are a participant?

- Which types of non-verbal communication do you think are most important to notice? To use?

- In which circumstances might non-verbal communication be different; in other words, what factors might affect the types of non-verbal communication being used?

Pronunciation and Other Verbal Cues

Pronunciation is an important part of participating in any type of interaction, so it obviously plays a role in discussions. Here are some pronunciation and language notes you should be familiar with and consider when you work with groups.

Hesitations

What do you do when you just do not know what to say? Earlier in this textbook, you learned phrases you can use to clarify or say when you don't understand. You also learned strategies that may help, such as paraphrasing. Sometimes, though, you just need a moment to collect your thoughts or frame what you want to say. Imagine a job interview in which the employer asks a question. You have no choice but to answer, but you want to think of your answer before you start speaking. Most listeners don't mind that you need a few moments before you begin. But if you think silently, offering no signs that you are thinking, they may not realize that you are "thinking." Non-verbal cues can help. For example, if you nod your head, tip your head, or touch your chin, all common signs that someone is thinking, the listener will know you are thinking. Unfortunately, these are of little help in certain settings, such as a classroom that has participants lined in rows and you can't see everyone's faces. These non-verbal cues can be of no help in what is becoming more and more popular—telephone interviews and meetings, even if those might be online, they are happening on small phone screens or with bad connections that hinder the communication. Therefore, giving some sort of verbal cue in conjunction with non-verbal cues is beneficial. The verbal cue doesn't have to be much; the key is that it is verbal and the listeners can hear it.

Some verbal cues you might hear are:

...like...	*That's a good question.*
Alright....	*Uhhh....*
Basically,...	*Umm.*
Give me a	*Well, it's hard to know where*
second.	*to start....*
Good question.	*Well....*
Hmmm.	*You know....*
Let me think....	*You see....*
Let's see....	

[other sounds—clicking or clucking tongue, *er, ah*]

Combinations are also possible:

Well, hmmm, give me a second....

Or you can hesitate before letting the listener know you are attempting an answer or giving your opinion:

Well, I'm not sure, but I think....

Note that sometimes a hesitation device could be extended:

Weeeeellllll....

One thing to remember is that hesitation devices are sometimes a sign of lacking knowledge or speaking skills, but NOT always. Sometimes they really are just a marker that you are framing your idea. It is often better to let the person know you heard them and are participating than not verbalizing anything at all. Always remember that saying something is better than worrying about perfect grammar or pronunciation.

TASK 24

Answer these questions with a partner.

1. Which hesitation devices do you think might be better than others? Why do you think so?

2. How many hesitation devices do you use? Could you use more or less? Have you noticed native speakers using hesitation devices?

3. How can you achieve a goal of using fewer hesitations?

Volume

Leaders and participants need to make sure they are speaking loudly enough that everyone can hear them. Leaders may ask participants to speak louder if someone can't hear. While you aren't presenting per se, everyone does need to hear you. Volume can also enhance your clarity or pronunciation.

Stress

Word Stress

Multi-syllabic words in English have one syllable that is stressed more than the others. The stress falls over the vowel in a word. You say the syllable louder, longer, and with a different pitch to stress it. There are many rules associated with word stress. For example, the stress in most words that end in *–al* fall on the third to last syllable.

> *ex-CEP-tion-al*   *CRI-ti-cal*

All the word stress rules can't be covered here, but consulting a good pronunciation book and familiarizing yourself with some general rules, such as stressing the first syllable of most two-syllable nouns (*CLI-mate* or *PRES-ent*) and the second syllable of most two-syllable verbs (*de-CIDE* or *pre-SENT*) can be helpful.

TASK 25

Make a list of words common in your field of study or words you struggle to say. Determine which syllable should be stressed.

TASK 26

Look up how to pronounce words with these suffixes in English. What are one or two sample words for each suffix?

Example:

   –ic   stress one syllable before the suffix   *classic/specific*

1.   *–tion / –sion*

2.   *–ity*

3.   *–phy*

4.   *–eer*

5.   *–ate*

6.   *–ible*

7.   *–ese*

8.   *–ify*

9.   *–ogy*

10. *–ize*

SENTENCE STRESS

In English, certain words in a sentence are emphasized more than others. Again, there are some general rules, but this also allows speakers to express which word they feel is the most important. Emphasize or give prominence to a certain word in a sentence. This helps your listeners understand the word or what you feel is the most important word in a statement. The word you stress can dramatically change the meaning of a sentence.

Compare these statements (capital letters indicate stress).

> I did not say you could come to the party. (Someone else said that.)
>
> I did NOT say that you could come to the party. (I deny saying that.)
>
> I did not SAY that you could come to the party. (But maybe I thought it.)
>
> I did not say that YOU could come to the party. (But I did say someone else could.)
>
> I did not say that you COULD come to the party. (Of course you can come to the party.)
>
> I did not say that you could COME to the party. (I said you could help plan the party.)
>
> I did not say that you could come to the PARTY. (I said you could come to the dinner.)

Like word stress, say the stressed word louder, longer, and with a higher pitch. In general, stress words that contain the most meaning, but do not stress words that are simply performing a function and don't hold as much meaning (unless, of course, one of those "small" words wasn't heard and caused a misunderstanding: *No, not the book ON the shelf. The one UNDER the shelf*). Function words are more for grammar and not the meaning. Again, saying something is better than not talking at all. Don't worry about perfect pronunciation.

Stress CONTENT words.	Do not stress FUNCTION words.
Nouns	Pronouns
Verbs	Prepositions
Adjectives	Conjunctions
Adverbs	Articles
Question words	Determiners
Negatives	Auxiliary verbs
Numbers or words you need for quality or quantity	Forms of the *be* verb

TASK 27

Can you think of a few examples for each item in the chart?

Stress CONTENT words.	Examples	Do not stress FUNCTION words.	Examples
nouns		pronouns	
verbs		prepositions	
adjectives		conjunctions	
adverbs		articles	
question words		determiners	
negatives		auxiliary verbs	
numbers or words you need for quality or quantity		forms of the *be* verb	

TASK 28

Read this short-term weather forecast from the National Weather Service. Which words would you stress? Then read it to partner. Ask your partner to mark which words they hear you stress. Reverse roles.

> SYNOPSIS...Weak high pressure will maintain dry weather through Friday morning. A cold front will return rain and mountain snow Friday afternoon and night. A cold upper trough will continue showers Saturday into Sunday morning as snow levels lower to 1500 to 2000 feet. Thunderstorms and small hail is possible with these showers. A series of surface fronts will result in chances for rain through the middle of next week.

> SHORT TERM...Today through Saturday Night...There are minimal clouds inland early this morning with low clouds and fog over the waters and along the immediate coast. Light onshore winds are advecting low marine clouds into some of the valleys of Pacific County and along the lower Columbia River. However, offshore winds are developing across NW Oregon as an inverted trough along the south Oregon coast is moving north. These offshore winds are keeping the low clouds just offshore of the central Oregon coast, and should limit the inland expansion of marine stratus for the north Oregon and south Washington coastal areas this morning.

> Further inland, satellite imagery shows signs of radiation fog and low clouds forming in the interior valleys of Lane County. The winds will likely be too light inland to prevent these low clouds from expanding into Linn County this morning. The low clouds should inland by mid-day, and inland temperatures should warm into the upper 50s this afternoon with some spots possibly peaking in the lower 60s.

Onshore winds return early Friday morning allowing marine clouds to move inland onto the coast. The winds will have a southerly component to it which may result in the marine clouds pushing into and up the Willamette Valley from the south. A slightly deeper marine layer will likely result in a slower clearing of the morning clouds. Mid and higher level clouds will fill in from the west Friday afternoon as a front approaches. The cloudy skies will result in less hours of sunshine on Friday for slightly cooler afternoon temperatures. Rain will move onto the coast late Friday afternoon pushing inland in the evening as the cold front moves inland.

Cooler air behind the front will lower snow levels below the Cascade passes Friday night into Saturday morning as an upper trough continues showers into the evening. The snow levels are expected to lower to around 2000 feet late Saturday morning. Models suggest that there will be enough instability to support a slight chance for thunderstorms along the coast Friday night and Saturday morning, and inland Saturday afternoon. Small hail is likely with these showers. The front will also support breezy south to southwest winds Friday night into Saturday morning.

From Friday night to Saturday afternoon, up to 2 inches of snow is possible for the higher elevations of the coast range and Cascade foothills, with 3 to 5 inches of snow expected for the Cascades. Rainfall totals of 0.5 to 0.75 inches is expected for the coast, coastal mountains and Cascade foothills (below 2000 feet), with around 0.25 inch of rain possible for the interior valleys.

Showers continue Saturday night as cooler air lowers snow levels down to around 1500 feet. The showers should become less frequent and widespread and limit the threat for accumulating snow.

From:
https://forecast.weather.gov/product.php?site=PQR&issuedby=
PQR&product=AFD&format=CI&version=1&glossary=1

> So You Want to Lead a Discussion
>
> - Did your partner mark the words you thought you stressed? What was the same? What was different?
>
> - Why might your partner not have heard the same thing you intended to say? What can you do to improve your stress patterns?
>
> - Did you correctly identify your partner's stresses? Why is it important to be able to hear someone's stresses when you are leading a discussion?

Pitch

Your voice should rise and fall when you speak. If you use a higher pitch, the statement is usually positive.

We covered a lot of content in today's discussion. (↑)

If you use a lower pitch, the statement is usually negative.

We didn't' come to a final decision. We'll have to revisit it later. (↓)

Tone

Tone expresses a speaker's attitude and conveys meaning behind the word choice. Even if you say the "right" words, if your tone is negative, it could hurt the interaction. Look at the example. Someone can be very happy about the final decision the group made; someone else might be disappointed about the decision.

Our decision is to use genetically modified food as our project topic.

TASK 29

For each of these statements you might say during a discussion, pronounce them using different stresses, pitches, and tones. Which way communicates your intent?

I'm sorry, but I don't think I understand what you meant.

So, can we all agree that our best option is to cover Fitzgerald's themes?

We have drifted off topic. Let's get back to the point.

To me, we should cover both the pros and cons.

Although the economy is important, I think we should focus on population issues.

So You Want to Lead a Discussion

- Think of things you have said or heard many times during a class discussion. Practice saying them with the appropriate stress, pitch, and tone.

4

Video Analysis

It is ideal to observe actual, live discussions. Attend seminars, workshops, conferences, guest speaker engagements, and panel discussions anytime you can. Pay close attention in class and during your own discussions, too. Take note of the language being used and the moves as they play out. It can also be helpful to watch created videos. They can help you analyze what is good and what is bad in a discussion.

For each video, click on the link at www.press. umich.edu/elt/compsite/leading and read the script for the mock discussion. Remember that a mock discussion is not authentic. These discussions are provided to help recognize language and moves. When you finish reading the script and watching the video, analyze and discuss by focusing on these tasks and questions.

1. Highlight the language speakers use to identify their purpose.
2. Write the number of the move each type of language belongs to.
3. What moves does this mock discussion use (Example 1, 2, 3, 4, 3, 4, 5, 6)? Does it work? Could it be better or worse?
4. Would you change any of the language? Add more? Use less? Explain.
5. How did the speakers make use of the pronunciation features discussed in this textbook? How did the speakers make use of non-verbal communication? Would you change anything?
6. Was this a successful discussion? Why or why not?
7. What roles did each person play? Did one lead more than the others? How were the roles (or shared roles) beneficial or detrimental?
8. Make a list of idioms or vocabulary you aren't familiar with. What do those words or phrases mean?

Video Analysis 1: Mock Discussion to Choose a Group Paper Topic

STUDENT 1: That was a good lecture on freedom of the press. Sounds like if there hadn't been freedom of the press, people wouldn't have found out about the Watergate scandal. This could be an interesting topic to research for our paper.

STUDENT 3: Yeah.

STUDENT 2: I agree. I think we should start by defining freedom of the press as the right to communicate through written forms, like magazines and newspapers and then talk about the role the *Washington Post* played in Nixon's resignation.

STUDENT 3: Well, wait. Before we move forward, I think we need to change that definition. Remember that freedom of the press also applies to electronic forms of media, like radio and television.

STUDENT 1: I'm positive we need to include online media too. You know? The internet.

STUDENT 3: Yeah.

STUDENT 2: Good points. I think a question we need to consider too is how much freedom the press should have.

STUDENT 1: I'm convinced that government information should remain private. Each government should decide what becomes public and what remains private.

STUDENT 3: Hmmm. Wait. I need to cut in. Are you saying that the *Post* should not have released that information about the Watergate scandal?

STUDENT 1: Well, kind of, yeah.

STUDENT 3: Well, listen, the people elect the president, right? So let me pose this question: If the people elect the president, then shouldn't they also have the right to know what the president is doing?

STUDENT 2: I think so. I think the *Post* had every right to report the Watergate scandal. My guess is that they thought the situation evolved into something more important than the other stories they were covering at the time because high-ranking officials were involved. Um, that made it, you know, a scandal, more than just a regular story.

STUDENT 1: Sorry, but I disagree. Wouldn't you agree that sometimes there can be too much information put out there?

STUDENT 2: Like when?

STUDENT 1: Well, like when details of some secret mission of some sort are revealed, which jeopardizes the mission, and all because the press thought it had the right to disseminate whatever it knows.

STUDENT 3: Well, excuse me. I see exactly where you're going, but I think we need to get back to Watergate. Otherwise, we're gonna just have too much information for the assignment.

STUDENT 1: Yeah, we'll have too much because the press printed too much!

STUDENT 2: Let me jump in here and offer a compromise. You're for complete freedom of the press [to Student 3] and you're for no freedom [to Student 1]?

STUDENT 1: No, let me clarify. Not no freedom. Just limited or restricted information related to the government.

STUDENT 2: Ok, so, I think we should define freedom of the press, talk about Watergate and the role of the press at that time and in that event, and then talk about different rules that might apply.

STUDENT 3: Such as?

STUDENT 2: Like sunshine laws or freedom of legislation laws. I'm pretty sure people can request government information through those. Um. Those might be different from the freedom of information laws. I'm not sure, so we'd have to check on that.

STUDENT 1: That's not a bad idea. How about if we all do an online search before we meet again.

STUDENTS 2 and 3: Ok.

STUDENT 3: That sounds good.

Video Analysis 2: Mock Discussion to Practice for a Test

STUDENT 1: Hey, when is the test?

STUDENT 2: It's on the 22nd.

STUDENT 3: Wait, the 22nd? Thursday?!

STUDENT 2: Oh, no, wait. I meant to say it's on Friday. Friday, the 23rd.

STUDENT 3: Ok, good. Well, that gives us one extra night to study.

STUDENT 1: Yeah, the instructor said we'll have to look at a painting and write about why we appreciate it.

STUDENT 2: Let's practice with the ones in the book. [opens book]

STUDENT 3: Great.

STUDENT 2: What about something by Rembrandt?

STUDENT 3: I really like that one. It's called "A Lady and Gentleman in Black." I love the way that the black and white clothing really stands out against that neutral background. Plus, with so little color, the painting is just so dramatic. Do you guys like this one?

STUDENT 1:[shrugs] Umm. Not really.

STUDENT 2: Uh, sort of. Personally, I like more color. What I'm trying to say is that there is only a little bit of red and pink in this one.

STUDENT 1: Hey, you know what? Actually this one is missing from a museum in Boston. Yeah, I was looking up another one and found out that it, and this Rembrandt and some others were stolen, too.

STUDENT 3: Really?

STUDENT 2: Oh, I heard about that too. It was the Gardner Museum in Boston. It happened more than 20 years ago. The biggest art theft in history. They still don't know where they went or where they are now.

STUDENT 1: [looking on computer] Hey, guess what? I just found another one that was stolen from the museum. It's a portrait of Rembrandt. Now, I really like portraits. They tell me what people looked like. Besides that, I can look at the subject's face and try to figure out what they were thinking. And this is one is a self-portrait, which makes it really interesting. Do you like it?

STUDENT 2: Uh-huh. I've always wondered, how do people someone paint themselves?

STUDENT 3: Well, here's what the TA told me. Basically, they use mirrors. Self-portraits have been around since the beginning of painting, but it wasn't until around the mid-15th century that self-portraits really became popular because of mirrors. Before that, mirrors just weren't good enough. Do you guys like, ah, this one?

STUDENT 2: Uh. It's OK. The mirror/self-portrait fact is an interesting tidbit. But I usually like paintings that are more colorful and less literal—if that's the right word. Umm, let me show you one I like. [opens book] This one by Manet. "Chez Tortoni." There's just something about this one that I really like. Manet was one of the Impressionists.

STUDENT 1: Oh, I've heard about the Impressionists. French, right?

STUDENT 2: Monet was probably the most famous, but, as a general rule, Manet did more paintings about people relaxing, like at cafés. "Chez Tortoni" is in a café. Typically, Monet did landscapes.

STUDENT 3: Hmmm. That's really interesting. I guess I didn't realize that.

STUDENT 2: See, I just like the way that, uh, Manet used green in this. I don't know what it was supposed to represent, but I like wondering about it.

STUDENT 1: Um, not me. True, this painting is more colorful, but I'd still vote for something else. In other words, I'd still pick self-portraits.

STUDENT 3: Yeah, and I'd still go with the Rembrandt.

STUDENT 2: Well, I guess this is what we are supposed to be doing, right? Appreciation varies person to person, and we're doing the right thing, right?

Video Analysis 3: Mock Discussion on an Assignment for a Class Talk

STUDENT 1: So, how do you like architecture class so far?

STUDENT 2: It's okay. Is it your major?

STUDENT 1: I haven't decided yet. You?

STUDENT 2: I don't think so, but in my country, there are many challenges in that field.

STUDENT 1: Which country are you from?

STUDENT 2: Beijing, China.

STUDENT 1: Oh! That's so cool! My dad had a business trip there two years ago, and our family got to tag along. It was amazing! I was so surprised at how friendly people were, and many people tried to, uh, speak a few English words to us.

STUDENT 2: Oh, wow! I haven't met any American student who has been to my country before.

STUDENT 1: Maybe we could pick a building in Beijing.

STUDENT 2: Uh huh. Yeah.

[STUDENT 3 enters and sits down.]

STUDENT 3: Hey, sorry I'm so late.

STUDENTS 1 and 2: Hi./Hey.

STUDENT 3: Yeah, parking was an absolute nightmare out there! What are you guys talking about?

STUDENT 2: My country. Anna's been there before.

STUDENT 3: Oh, ok. So you haven't started the assignment yet? Well, I think we're supposed to decide on a building to discuss. Any ideas?

STUDENT 1: Yeah, we talked about a building in China. But, is it okay if were view the guidelines on the assignment first? That would really help me.

STUDENT 2: Yeah, sure. I have it here in my notes—choose a structure, research its history, take notes on its design, and present that to class. Why don't we choose one of the tallest buildings in the world?

STUDENT 3: Um. Wait. Excuse me. Don't you think that a lot of other people are going to do that too?

STUDENT 2: Well, I'm not sure about that.

STUDENT 3: I'm sorry. I'm not saying it's a bad idea; it's just, I think that a lot of other groups are going to do it too. Maybe we can talk about a particular type of building. Like a house, or a museum, or an office building?

STUDENT 2: But I don't think that's as interesting as focusing on a really tall building though.

STUDENT 3: Well, I don't know. The professor brought up a whole bunch of really interesting facts about those other buildings. Like, I thought the stuff he said about hotels was really cool, even though they weren't the tallest.

STUDENT 2: But we have to be able to talk a lot about a building. If it's tall, if it's big, that will help us, right?

STUDENT 3: Yeah.

STUDENT 1: Excuse me. How about a compromise? The actual assignment says "structure," right? We could pick, uh, the tallest structure, like, a, a, like a radio or television tower or even a sightseeing tower like the Space Needle in Seattle or the Eiffel Tower.

STUDENT 3: Wow, yeah, I mean, we could look into doing a project on the tallest structure instead of the tallest building.

STUDENT 2: Yeah. I got a little frustrated. That's a good idea.

STUDENT 1: Good. I'll research the CN Tower in Toronto, Ontario.

STUDENT 3: Um, hey, while you're doing that, could you also do some research on that one tower in China that we talked about in class? You guys wanted to do something about a structure in China, right?

STUDENT 1: Ok. Yeah. That one's cool! How, uh, do you spell it again?

STUDENT 2: Um, it's G-u-a-n-g-z-h-o-u.

STUDENT 3: Ok, and I can also do some research on the Eiffel Tower. I mean, that's an oldie, but it's still a goodie.

STUDENT 2: Yeah. When was that one built?

STUDENT 3: You know, I don't know that, but I'll check on it.

STUDENT 2: Yeah, and I'll check some of my, my, the telecommunications tower in my country, maybe one in Russia.

STUDENT 1: Uh, do you want to get, guys, uh, together tomorrow to review what we found?

STUDENT 2: Um. I can't. I have class. But maybe we can, I can do after 4.

STUDENT 3: Okay, well, that works for me. Um, you guys are going to have to excuse me. I need to run to another class. So, bye.

STUDENTS 1 and 2: OK.

[STUDENT 3 gets up and leaves the scene.]

STUDENT 1: Hey, Serena, do you think that maybe sometime we could grab some coffee and talk more about China. There's a few things I am really curious about but have never had anyone to ask.

STUDENT 2: Yeah, sure. I'd like that.

Video Analysis 4: Mock Discussion on Choosing a Topic for a Speech

STUDENT 1: Okay, so for the assignment in Political Science class, we have to choose one of the city's mayoral candidates whose platform we like and prepare a campaign speech for him or her.

STUDENT 2: Well, maybe we should all start by saying which candidate we like.

STUDENT 1: That's a good idea. You start.

STUDENT 3: I'll start. I like Andrew Collins because he has a father who worked for the city for 20 years.

STUDENT 2: But having a father who works as a government employee doesn't make you a good candidate. I think that Deborah Michaels would be a better choice. She was a city council member, and she was also the city manager. She has a lot of experience working with others at city hall. And, she also publicly supports hospitals and parks, so therefore, she is promoting health care and the environment.

STUDENT 1: I agree, but don't you think we need to focus on their views on education? I mean, we are students in an educational system. So, Nathaniel Williams is a candidate who has a college degree in education, he taught for the public school system, and he said he wants our school system to be the best in the state.

STUDENT 3: I like your idea of considering viewpoints, but I think we should focus on more than one issue here. How about unemployment and the environment? Andrew Collins has a plan for both those issues. His plane will lower the city's unemployment by nine percent.

STUDENT 2: No way. That's impossible. How . . . What's his plan for that?

STUDENT 3: That's not impossible. He's going to bring new companies, so there will be more jobs in the city.

STUDENT 2: But, how? Has he said how he's going to do that? I mean, I think we need to focus on someone with more experience. He doesn't seem like he's very qualified.

STUDENT 3: I want to talk about Collins some more here. Um. Not only did his father work for the city, but he himself was also a government employee. He worked in the Department of Public Safety. He cares about the crime rate!

STUDENT 1: Right. Crime's important. Uh, but what other departments did he work for? Now, I mentioned Williams because he has experience in education. And that should be our focus right now. The schools just lost budget and, and, and the funding really needs to go there.

STUDENT 2: You're entitled to your opinion, but I think we need a candidate that has a little more experience and a comprehensive platform. I think Williams could get my vote.

STUDENT 3: Really? [pause]. I suppose I can support Williams just for the purposes of this assignment.

STUDENT 1: Okay. That's great. So, let's research Williams, and we'll focus on the topic as well that you're interested in . . . crime, and I'm sure you guys will find that his viewpoint is very well-rounded.

Video Analysis 5: Mock Discussion to Think of a Business Idea

STUDENT 1: Well, I'm kinda excited about this assignment. Sounds like we can be a little creative.

STUDENT 2 : Yeah. Yeah. It's very cool that the team with the best idea gets to enter its idea in the department's new aspiring entrepreneur contest.

STUDENT 3: We need something beyond great.

STUDENT 1: Um. How about a restaurant? I think we can make a pizzeria since all college students love pizza.

STUDENT 2: What's innovative about that?

STUDENT 3: Well, we can make it pizza with a twist. Like an extra healthy pizza. A pizza with only vegetables and a really thin crust.

STUDENT 2: That is an idea. But, there's so much competition with restaurants. I think retail is a better choice. I think I'd rather start a bookstore. People are always wandering in and out of bookstores. We all need to buy books. And I think the key is to make ours a trading store. You bring a book, you get to take one with you. We'd never have to worry about stock!

STUDENT 3: I'll grant you that, but, how would we create any revenue? And don't you think we need to consider that anything retail is gonna completely run the judges away? We're going to need money just to start off the stock for that bookstore. We need to find something that the judges won't mind starting to fund off the ground. Hmm.

STUDENT 1: Yep. I agree.

STUDENT 3: I think we need something creative that'll need no start-up money. I was thinking of something along the lines of clothing.

STUDENT 2: Like what specifically?

STUDENT 3: Well, I was thinking . . . plastic shoe covers. Okay, it's always getting wet around here, and by the time people get to class, their shoes are soaking wet. People will love not having to walk around with an extra pair of shoes in their back pocket, or their book bags. And we'd actually be saving people money because they wouldn't have to buy new shoes because they'd have to replace the old shoes. Yeah, the shoe covers could be sold in boxes of ten or twelve. And we could offer a buy one, get one free coupon.

STUDENT 1: Oooh, that sounds great to me. I can totally go with that idea. What we can do is we can propose that they be made out of the same material like plastic bags. Then they can be recyclable. And we can toss them into the nearest recycle bin when we go to class. Seriously, that's a really good idea.

STUDENT 2: But then everybody would have to carry around a box of recyclable shoe covers in their backpack.

STUDENT 1:Hmm. Yeah. Well, maybe we should go back to my restaurant idea. Like we have a lot of room for creativity. And maybe we can decorate the inside like a place, like a beach or a hot vacation spot. Then we can say there's always a place to come in without the rain.

STUDENT 2:You could do the same thing with a bookstore. And we could have a café as part of the bookstore.

STUDENT 3:Hmm. Even though that may be true, we're still going to need funding from judges. I think we need to think in terms of something smaller.

STUDENT 1: I can go with part of the idea. Like escaping the rain is great. But why don't we find something more campus-related? How about a waterproof notebook?

STUDENT 3:Hmm. Everyone recognizes that it's always wet around here in the winter. Something waterproof may actually be a great idea.

STUDENT 2: Okay. You win. A bookstore or a restaurant would never get funded. And I think college students are super vain; they would never wear shoe covers anyway. I vote we go with the waterproof notebook idea.

STUDENT 1, STUDENT 3: [Assorted murmurs and non-verbal cues.]

Video Analysis 6: Mock Discussion on an Astronomy Project

STUDENT 1: So, we need to figure out which mission to present to the other groups. Any ideas?

STUDENT 2: It's kind of a tough decision. I mean, the instructor talked about so many.

STUDENT 3: Well, I'd say Apollo is the clear winner here. President Kennedy believed in that one really strongly and I think it put the first man on the moon.

STUDENT 2: Perhaps higher consideration should be given to Explorer. This was America's first artificial satellite.

STUDENT 1: I see both of your points, but I think that we should choose a current mission because both of yours are in the past.

STUDENT 2: I see where you're coming from on this one. Is there a mission you would suggest?

STUDENT 1: I suppose priority should be given to Aura because it's about the environment of the Earth's atmosphere, and I think that's a really hot topic right now.

STUDENT 2: I like the thought of using a current mission, but I'm not sure I would use that topic because it's a scientific mission. We probably don't know enough about it. I think we should consider using Constellation. This is the program that plans not only to send humans to the moon, but to Mars, and other places.

STUDENT 3: Well, I guess I can be swayed away from a mission in the past. But if we're going to go in that direction, maybe we can consider something in the future. Take Juno.

STUDENT 1: What did the teacher say about that one again?

STUDENT 3: Um, I'm pretty sure that's the one that's going to explore Jupiter.

STUDENT 2: I'm sorry I can't remember either. But I think the teacher said something about the international space station.

STUDENT 1: I don't have that in my notes, but I think that's, um, there was a future mission planned to the international space station. Who'd like to use that as our topic?

STUDENT 2: Well, I'm not sure about a future mission, but I think it's a good choice because it had past missions, still has current missions, and probably will have a future mission.

STUDENT 3: Yeah, but even so, I'm not sure we should choose something that addresses all three time periods. After all, we have ten minutes to discuss this, and that's not much time.

STUDENT 1: Well, I couldn't tell you which time period each thing happened in, but I could look it up. We should focus on one time period first. I think a current mission would be most appealing.

STUDENT 3: Okay. Can we all agree on that?

STUDENT 1: Yep.

STUDENT 2: I think so, but I still feel Constellation is a good choice because people are really fascinated about the thought of going to outer space and beyond.

STUDENT 1: I still strongly believe that Aura is the best choice. It's about the environment.

STUDENT 3: Hey, um, if we want to talk about the environment, maybe, um, SERVIR. . .is that how you say that, well, maybe that's an ideal choice. Um. I think that's the one that's going to integrate satellite data with equipment on the ground to forecast environmental changes.

STUDENT 2: I'd like to put in a bid for one more possibility—what about the Cassini-Huygens Mission that plans to study Saturn. Let's tackle something entirely new here and surprise everybody in the audience.

STUDENT 1: Well, we've had a lot of suggestions for the past and the future, but the most for present missions. So maybe we should think about it and mee tafter class.

STUDENT 2, STUDENT 3: [Murmurs of agreement.]

5

Suggested Group Activities

Leading a Discussion (Leader)

Plan to lead the class for _____ minutes on [DATE]. In advance of your date, complete this checklist and prepare notes.

_____ Choose your topic.

_____ Narrow your topic.

_____ Choose a kickoff question.

_____ Prepare background information (if necessary)

_____ Prepare two to five sub-questions.

_____ Anticipate questions and comments.

_____ Prepare to manage the speakers personalities, the time, and the content.

_____ Summarize throughout (as needed) and at the end.

Leading a Discussion (Participant)

You will participate in class discussions led by your classmates.

For each discussion, be prepared to complete this checklist.

_____ Review phrasing you will need (example: opinions, agreeing, disagreeing...)
_____ Actively listen.
_____ Actively participate.
_____ Ask questions.

See sample rubrics in Appendix 3.

Panel Discussion

Plan to participate in a panel discussion with a group on [DATE].

In advance of your date, complete this checklist and prepare notes.

_____ Brainstorm topics.
_____ Choose and formulate a topic.
_____ Choose a moderator.
_____ Choose panelists to speak on different aspects of the topic.
_____ Prepare for the general procedure:
- moderator introduces topic and panelists
- moderator provides introduction of topic and panelists
- moderator poses question

- panelists discuss and make comments on each other's points
- moderator controls topic and panelists
- moderator briefly summarizes

_____ Prepare for the Q & A from the audience.

_____ Prepare notes. Note: Panels are like conversations in front of an audience. They do not require prepared presentations or serious research, but some preparation is helpful to familiarize yourself with the topic, be prepared for questions, and plan points you want to make.

_____ Review phrasing you will need.

_____ Manage the time limits. (20 to 30 minutes to present information; 15 to 20 minutes for a forum period in which the audience will answer questions or make comments)

Other Projects

1. Explain a concept in your field to the rest of the class (non-specialists or academics NOT in your field).

2. Debate a hot topic or current issue.

3. Plan a poster or overview of your research for a research group meeting or poster session.

4. Conduct a survey, collect data, and prepare a presentation about the results and your conclusions.

5. Prepare a group presentation on a topic of your choice and then lead a class discussion.

6. Prepare a SWOT analysis about a company you create or a real-life company and present it for discussion.

7. Read an article or case study to discuss with the rest of the class.

8. Prepare a 3MT® and field the Q&A.

9. Watch or attend a panel or seminar on campus. Prepare a report or watch a video of it with the class. Discuss the speakers' phrasing and content.

10. Record any projects for self, peer, or instructor evaluation.

Appendixes

Appendix 1: NASA Ranking Chart for Task 15

Items from Spaceship	NASA's Reasoning	NASA's Ranking	Independent Ranking	Error Points	Group Ranking	Error Points
Box of matches	No oxygen on the moon; virtually worthless	15				
Food concentrate	Efficient means of supplying energy	4				
Fifty feet of nylon rope	Useful in scaling cliffs, tying injured together	6				
Parachute silk	Protection from sun's rays	8				
Solar-powered portable heating unit	Not needed unless on dark side of the moon	13				
Two .45 caliber pistols	Propulsion	11				
One case of dehydrated milk	Bulkier duplication of food concentrate	12				
Two 100-pound tanks of oxygen	Most pressing survival need	1				
Stellar map (of the moon's constellations)	Primary means of navigation	3				
Self-inflating life raft	CO_2 bottle may be used for propulsion	9				
Magnetic compass	Magnetic field on moon not polarized; worthless	14				
Five gallons of water	Replacement of liquids	2				
Signal flares	Signal when mother ship is sighted	10				
First-aid kit containing injection needles	For vitamins, medications, etc.	7				
Solar-powered FM receiver-transmitter	Communication with mother ship	5				
				Independent Total		Group Total

Error points are the absolute difference between your rankings and NASA's.

Scoring guide: 0-25 excellent, 26-32 good, 33-45 average, 46-55 fair, 56-70 poor, 71-112 very poor use of earth-bound logic!

Appendix 2: Robert's Rules of Order

Parliamentary Procedure for Meetings Robert's Rules
of Order is the standard for facilitating discussions and
group decision-making. Copies of the rules are available at most bookstores. Although they may seem long
and involved, having an agreed upon set of rules makes
meetings run easier. Robert's Rules will help your group
have better meetings, not make them more difficult.
Your group is free to modify them or find another suit-
able process that encourages fairness and participation,
unless your bylaws state otherwise.

Here are the basic elements of Robert's Rules, used
by most organizations:

1. Motion: To introduce a new piece of
   business or propose a decision or action, a
   motion must be made by a group member
   ("I move that......") A second motion must
   then also be made (raise your hand and say,
   "I second it.") After limited discussion the
   group then votes on the motion. A majority
   vote is required for the motion to pass (or
   quorum as specified in your bylaws.)
2. Postpone Indefinitely: This tactic is used
   to kill a motion. When passed, the motion
   cannot be reintroduced at that meeting. It
   may be brought up again at a later date. This
   is made as a motion ("I move to postpone
   indefinitely..."). A second is required. A
   majority vote is required to postpone the
   motion under consideration.

3. Amend: This is the process used to change a motion under consideration. Perhaps you like the idea proposed but not exactly as offered. Raise your hand and make the following motion: "I move to amend the motion on the floor." This also requires a second. After the motion to amend is seconded, a majority vote is needed to decide whether the amendment is accepted. Then a vote is taken on the amended motion. In some organizations, a "friendly amendment" is made. If the person who made the original motion agrees with the suggested changes, the amended motion may be voted on without a separate vote to approve the amendment.

4. Commit: This is used to place a motion in committee. It requires a second. A majority vote must rule to carry it. At the next meeting the committee is required to prepare a report on the motion committed. If an appropriate committee exists, the motion goes to that committee. If not, a new committee is established.

5. Question: To end a debate immediately, the question is called (say "I call the question") and needs a second. A vote is held immediately (no further discussion is allowed). A two-thirds vote is required for passage. If it is passed, the motion on the floor is voted on immediately.

6. Table: To table a discussion is to lay aside
   the business at hand in such a manner that
   it will be considered later in the meeting or
   at another time ("I make a motion to table
   this discussion until the next meeting. In the
   meantime, we will get more information so
   we can better discuss the issue.") A second is
   needed and a majority vote required to table
   the item being discussed.
7. Adjourn: A motion is made to end the
   meeting. A second motion is required.
   A majority vote is then required for the
   meeting to be adjourned (ended).

   Note: If more than one motion is proposed,
   the most recent takes precedence over the
   ones preceding it.

For example if #6, a motion to table the discussion,
is proposed, it must be voted on before #3, a motion to
amend, can be decided.

In a smaller meeting, like a committee or board
meeting, often only four motions are used: ·

To introduce (motion.)
To change a motion (amend.)
To adopt (accept a report without discussion.)
To adjourn (end the meeting.)

Remember, these processes are designed to ensure
that everyone has a chance to participate and to share
ideas in an orderly manner. Parliamentary procedure

should not be used to prevent discussion of important issues.

TIPS IN PARLIAMENTARY PROCEDURE

This summary will help you determine when to use the actions described in Robert's Rules.

- A main motion must be moved, seconded, and stated by the chair before it can be discussed.
- If you want to move, second, or speak to a motion, stand and address the chair.
- If you approve the motion as is, vote for it.
- If you disapprove the motion, vote against it.
- If you approve the idea of the motion but want to change it, amend it or submit a substitute for it.
- If you want advice or information to help you make your decision, move to refer the motion to an appropriate quorum or committee with instructions to report back.
- If you feel they can handle it better than the assembly, move to refer the motion to a quorum or committee with power to act.
- If you feel that there the pending question(s) should be delayed so more urgent business can be considered, move to lay the motion on the table.
- If you want time to think the motion over, move that consideration be deferred to a certain time.

- If you think that further discussion is unnecessary, move the previous question.
- If you think that the assembly should give further consideration to a motion referred to a quorum or committee, move the motion be recalled.
- If you think that the assembly should give further consideration to a matter already voted upon, move that it be reconsidered.
- If you do not agree with a decision rendered by the chair, appeal the decision to the assembly.
- If you think that a matter introduced is not germane to the matter at hand, a point of order may be raised.
- If you think that too much time is being consumed by speakers, you can move a time limit on such speeches.
- If a motion has several parts, and you wish to vote differently on these parts, move to divide the motion.

https://archive.fisheries.noaa.gov/afsc/Education/Activities/PDFs/SBSS_Lesson6_roberts_rules_of_order.pdf

Appendix 3: Rubrics

Leading a Discussion (Leader)

Task	+ (exceeds expectations) √ (meets expectations) - (below expectations)	Comments
Topic		
Kickoff question		
Background information		
Sub-questions		
Managed content		
Managed personalities		
Managed time		
Used appropriate phrasing		
Summarized		
Volume		
Eye contact		
General pronunciation notes		
General vocabulary notes		
General non-verbal communication notes		
General grammar notes		

Leading a Discussion (Participant)

Task	+ (exceeds expectations) √ (meets expectations) - (below expectations)	Comments
Participated in all discussions		
Actively listened		
Used appropriate phrasing		
Asked questions		
Volume		
Eye contact		
General pronunciation notes		
General vocabulary notes		
General non-verbal communication notes		
General grammar notes		

Leading a Discussion Peer Feedback Form

Name of student leading the discussion: _____

_____

Name of student providing the feedback: _____

_____

Positive notes: _____

_____

Constructive suggestions: _____

_____

Liked/Disliked topic because: _____

_____

Other notes: _____

_____

Panel Discussion (Moderator)

Task	+ (exceeds expectations) √ (meets expectations) - (below expectations)	Comments
Introduction of topic		
Introduction of panelists		
Background information		
Maintained flow		
Used appropriate phrasing		
Managed time		
Summarized		
Volume		
Eye contact		
General pronunciation notes		
General vocabulary notes		
General non-verbal communication notes		
General grammar notes		

Panel Discussion (Panelist)

Task	+ (exceeds expectations) √ (meets expectations) - (below expectations)	Comments
Contributed equally		
Contributions were relevant and important		
Background information		
Answered when called on		
Jumped in as necessary		
Used appropriate phrasing		
Volume		
Eye contact		
General pronunciation notes		
General vocabulary notes		
General non-verbal communication notes		
General grammar notes		

EXTRA READING

Barkley, E.F., Cross, K.P., & Major, C.H. (2005). *Collaborative learning techniques*. San Francisco: Jossey-Bass.

Johnson, D. W., Johnson, R. T., & Smith, K. (1991). *Cooperative learning: Increasing college faculty instructional productivity. (ASHE-ERIC Higher Education Report No. 4)*. Washington, DC: George Washington University School of Education and Human Development.

Lockwood, R.B., (2018). *Speaking in social contexts: Communication for life and study in the United States*. Ann Arbor: University of Michigan Press.

Lockwood, R.B., (2019). *Office hours: What every university student needs to know*. Ann Arbor: University of Michigan Press.

Millis, B. J., & Cottell, P. G., Jr. (1998). *Cooperative learning for higher education faculty*. American Council on Education, Series on Higher Education. Phoenix: The Oryx Press.

Smith, K. A. (1996). Cooperative learning: Making "group work" work. In Sutherland, T. E., & Bonwell, C. C. (Eds.), *Using active learning in college classes: A range of options for faculty, New Directions for Teaching and Learning* No. 67.

Swales, J., & Feak, C. (2012). *Academic Writing for Graduate Students (3rd ed.)*. Ann Arbor: University of Michigan Press.